IMAGES
of England

PONTELAND

Main Street in 1904 showing West Farm (now Safeway) in the background next to the Albion Temperance Hotel (now Mackley & Studdart, Michael's, and others), The Seven Stars, Caughey's shop and post office (now HSBC Bank) and Caughey's Temperance Hotel (now Blockbuster Video). Mrs Shiells is standing in the doorway of the post office (with Albert Shiells in her arms) talking to Edward Jameson. W. Caughey is crossing the road in front of Edith Charlton with W. Brown and James Caughey, saddler, standing on the right in front of E. Jameson's shop.

Flooding of Main Street on 27 February 1900, viewed from the old bridge with The Coates Institute and Reading Room (now Your Move estate agent) to the right and West Farm in the background. Note the telegraph poles, but no electricity. The lamp on the bridge was probably oil or acetylene. From left to right: George Edward Henderson, Jack Brown, Charlie Wilkinson, Billy Bates (extreme right).

IMAGES
of England

PONTELAND

Compiled by
John Turner

TEMPUS

Tempus Publishing Limited
The Mill, Brimscombe Port,
Stroud, Gloucestershire, GL5 2QG

ISBN 0 7524 1806 8

Typesetting and origination by
Tempus Publishing Limited
Printed in Great Britain by
Midway Colour Print, Wiltshire

Looking east from the bridge with the entrance to the old Methodist chapel on the immediate right next to Jameson's shop and nursery during the flood of 1900. Note the Tudor-style building, with spire, in the background which was built in 1899 as a meeting place by the Cyclists' Touring Club.

Contents

Main Street under water in 1900, looking east towards Jameson's corner shop with the roof of The Diamond visible in the background. The policeman to the left stands in front of an abandoned Royal Mail Coach.

Acknowledgements

I am very grateful to my wife Pat for her patience, understanding and encouragement and I wish to record my gratitude to: Keith Robertson LRPS for his help and enthusiasm, Ponteland History Society for their permission to use archive material, Anthony Durkin and Revd David Hannan for allowing me to use material from their respective publications *Gods Orchard* and *A Goodly Heritage*. I would also like to thank: the late Kathleen Armstrong, Bryan Ashford, Liz and John Scott-Batey, Alan Bainbridge, Edith and John Banks, Mrs Nancy Blaylock, Michael Brown, Mrs Helen Brown, Mrs Cherry, Norman Cowan, Mrs Elsie Cowell, Barry Cowell, Bob Cowen, Mrs Mary Craven, Margaret and Bill Crow, Marjorie Dodds, Dick Dodsworth, Dulcie and Stan Dytham, Mr and Mrs Donald Elsmore, John English, Frank Harrington, Joan and Tom Harrison, Miss Mollie Henderson, Brian Hepple, Jack Heron, Liz and Ken Hogg, Brian and Isabel Jameson, the late Bill Johnson, Ronnie Johnson, Peter Kenyon, Bernard Long, David Marshall, Father Melia, Pat and Maurice Milburn, Mrs Catherine M. Parker, Tony Quinn, Mrs Margaret Robinson, Mrs V. Scott, Frank Smith, Ronnie Stobbs, Michael Taylor, John Thomson, June Thompson, Mrs Heather Tingey, Desmond Walton, Geoff and Dorothy Warner, Jack and the late Barbara White, Mrs Hazel Whitehead, Mrs May Woolley and Hew Wright, who have either provided photographs and memorabilia for my use, or helped with the indentification of people and places. If I have overlooked anyone then I offer my sincere apologies.

Introduction

This book is a lasting tribute to the help and encouragement I have received from Ponteland Local History Society and the many local people who have helped in its compilation. They have made their collections of photographs and memorabilia available to me and have given their time to share their recollections of events and people. Without their help this project would not have been possible and I have found it a humbling experience at times to be entrusted with such valuable and personal material. Much of the material, teased out of tin boxes and plastic bags in loft spaces, has been hidden away for many years and this project has provided the opportunity for it to be shared with others. There are some photographs which I have been unable to include because of publication or copyright restrictions and I do hope that the contributors will excuse their omission. I have met some very interesting people in preparing this publication and I trust they consider that their effort has been well rewarded.

Photographs are unique in the way they record people, events, and the changes which take place around us and I have included, with only a few digressions, only those photographs which have not generally been widely used in other publications. Those which have been repeated are included because of their historic significance and relevance to a particular section. I have made no attempt to produce a narrative covering the history of Ponteland, as this has been done by others in the past, but have set out to compile a collection which provides an insight into its growth and development and which will kindle sparks of recognition. I have endeavoured to use only photographs which could be dated and identified in detail but this has not always been possible. I would welcome contributions of additional information or corrections where I have erred.

The collection as presented is a small representation of the people, places and events in and around Ponteland over the last 100 years or so. There are numerous untold stories behind each photograph and I would regard the publication as successful if it motivates and encourages others to research, uncover, and record some of these for future generations. We are all guilty of putting off the day to ask questions about people, changes and events of the past and we suddenly find that it is too late. We never have the time to annotate our photographs and consequently the detail is, at worst, lost forever or, at best, requires a major commitment to research. There are many collections in storage which are considered by their holders to be of limited interest and I hope that this publication convinces those collectors that there is a genuine interest in sharing their material.

A number of families living in Ponteland today have ancestral connections in the area dating back for many years, in some cases centuries, and most have played significant roles in the development and evolution of the community. While the buildings and the evidence of the physical changes which have taken place are interesting for reflection, it is the people of the community who introduce and control those changes. They are the heart which supports the vibrant life of the community and without this it will fail. It is hoped that the photographs and accompanying text will not only serve to remind us of these changes but will also demonstrate the important roles that people have played. In some instances there is no longer physical evidence available to identify what things were really like and the photographs serve as a permanent and accurate reminder.

A 'tourist', travelling in the Woolsington area in the late eighteenth century, reported: 'The prospect over this part of the County at the turnpike bar [Kenton Bar perhaps], is so extraordinary, that I cannot forbear pointing it out to future ramblers. Ponteland is seated in the depth of the vale, shrouded with a pretty grove; Esland (Eland) Hall crowns the right hand eminence, beyond which the elegant house of Gosforth [perhaps the white freestone Gosforth House of the Brandlings], surrounded by rising plantations, fills the more distant landscape; the neat house at Beanridge [probably Benridge] to the left, contrasted by Berwick town [Berwick Hills], of Scotch aspect, whose black thatched cottages stretch along the neighbouring hill. One of the wings of Mr Ogle's house at Kirkley is seen through the trees, the white front, and deep coloured shade of the plantations, forming an agreeable mixture. The town of Ogle stands on an eminence in front, over which Whalton is seen, and the whole background is formed by the rugged rocks of Rothbury, which give a rough and distant horizon.' This early account sets the scene of the very rural location of Ponteland and its parish, prior to the visual intrusion of the airport and the urban sprawl from the city.

John Turner
May 1999

One

As It Was

The changes in Ponteland have at times been, though evolutionary, very subtle and almost unnoticeable. It is only the photographic evidence of the past that reminds us of the changes that have taken place. Some of these have clearly been for the better, however, there are some legacies from the 1960s which are perhaps best overlooked.

Despite early conjecture that 'Ponteland' was a derivation of the Roman Pons Aelli this was rightfully later attributed to Newcastle upon Tyne. There are many other ancient documentary references such as Pont-Island, Pont-Eland, Pont Ealand and Pont Esland which clearly reflect the nature of its position, close to the river Pont and surrounded by low lying fen or marsh lands.

Frequent flooding was a common feature of the Pont and it is recorded that the village was inundated several times in the 1800s. Particularly dramatic examples occurred in 1900 and 1903 and these were recorded by Robert Charlton, an amateur photographer living in Ponteland, who was also responsible for many of the photographs of other early village scenes. Some of these, from original mounts and glass plates, appear within this publication. It was not until the early 1990s that major flood defence works were undertaken to restrain the Pont.

The basic layout of the village, centred on the line of the 1830 Ponteland turnpike road to Scotland and its crossing of the river, has changed very little over the past 200 years or so, although individual buildings have been subject to alteration, restoration or demolition. The principal occupations during these years were initially very closely associated with agriculture although there was limited employment in mining and brick making. The Meadowfield Industrial Estate has introduced a range of new businesses over the years and development of the computer industry at the east end of Bell Villas seems appropriate as we approach the Millennium.

During the nineteenth century the population of the parish remained fairly static and despite the rapid developments of road and rail transport, and some early twentieth-century growth, it was not until the 1950s and '60s that Ponteland began to realise its full potential.

A late nineteenth-century view clearly shows The Diamond with only two storeys. The ramp evident between the Toll House and the old bridge suggests that this was perhaps the approach to an earlier ford crossing of the river Pont.

A similar view taken from an early 1900s postcard shows little change apart from the additional storey to The Diamond.

Perhaps now one of the most common views of Ponteland and certainly one which has been captured many times over the years by local artists. This view from around 1900 shows Callerton Lane and The Diamond with only three attic windows in the additional third floor. The proprietor's name, M. J. Wilkinson, is prominently displayed.

The fourth attic window is pictured here, it probably dates from around 1908. Note the hay cart by the river and the pile of rubble, which is probably from the rebuilding of the Methodist chapel.

The old bridge, Coates Endowed School and St Mary's church, *c.* 1908.

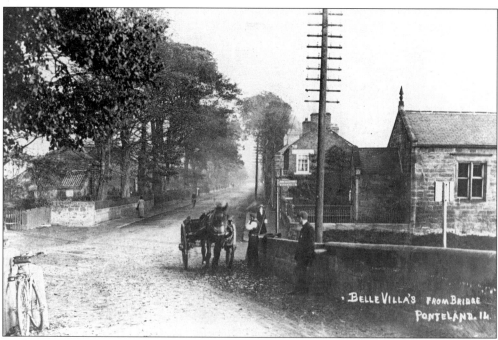

Looking east down Bell Villas from the bridge, *c.* 1907. The old chapel is pictured, along with the veranda that was added to Jameson's shop and the gable end of the adjoining property.

Looking east down Bell Villas, *c.* 1900. This shows the position of the cyclists' meeting house and the unpaved road surface.

The Diamond and smithy, *c.* 1908. The blacksmith's sycamore tree, which was the cause of a public outcry when it was taken down in 1978 for safety reasons, is clearly evident here.

Blacksmith's inspection with onlookers in traditional pose. The dates indicate that this was perhaps a sixtieth year anniversary.

A post-1907 postcard view with children in 'Sunday best' outside the new chapel. The signpost indicates the direction of High Callerton and Newburn.

This early 1900s view up a narrow North Road shows The Coates Institute, a glimpse of the rectory and The Blackbird, out of sight to the far left. The additional poles suggest that electricity has been installed.

The Blackbird, c. 1910. Robert Deuchar Ltd was the proprietor at this time. The bearded gentlemen and the three children have walked from, or are walking to, the chapel shown on page 14.

A postcard view of St Mary's church, as seen from The Blackbird, *c.* 1910. This also shows carts belonging to Henderson (the builders) on North Road.

Looking east along Main Street, *c.* 1910. Pictured are the Albion Temperance Hotel, The Seven Stars, the tearooms and Caughey's shop (adjacent to the telegraph pole). The proprietor of The Seven Stars was R.P. Hogg Esq.

The entrance to Caughey's sweet shop, *c.* 1910. Pedestrian protection to the telegraph pole, which also appears on page 16, is clearly evident.

Looking west along Main Street, *c.* 1900. Neasham House (12 Main Street) is on the immediate right; Some of the neighbouring cottages have since been demolished. On the left is part of West Farm with the West End smithy in the distance.

An early 1900s view at the rear of West Farm to the south of Main Street looking north, with the old brewery chimney, behind The Seven Stars, just off the picture to the right. The south-facing rooftop of Neasham House can be seen to the left of the copse of trees, which surround the Pele Tower and vicarage.

The front of the nineteenth-century cottages, adjoining the West End smithy, which occupied the site of the present NatWest Bank.

Henry Stobert stands outside his father's original shop in West Road in the late 1800s. This was subsequently converted back into residential accommodation when the new shop and warehouse were built adjoining the property in the early 1900s.

Looking east along West Road, c. 1905. The rail bridge is visible in the distance just beyond the West End smithy on the right (now Snaith's butchers shop). The river can be seen to the extreme right with the railway embankment in the background. Anthony and Barbara Stobbs had earlier held the tenancy of The Windmill Inn, which stood just beyond the first telegraph pole.

A postcard view down North Road, c. 1910. Temporary huts at the back of No. 26 (the home of James Jameson) were the accommodation for Castle Ward RDC until 1936 when they moved to No. 7.

The New Bridge, Ponteland. 7156

A view of the new bridge and The Diamond, c. 1926. Note the new Co-op building (now Bottoms Up) which was built next to the blacksmith's house in Bell Villas.

A late 1920s view of Main Street from the bridge, showing Lloyds Bank and part of the Temperance Café. The old Albion Temperance Hotel had by this time been converted to become Thompson's Garage.

Looking back east along Main Street in the late 1920s, with Jameson's Garage just in view to the left.

A late 1920s view of North Road showing the Coates School to the right and The Blackbird Gardens immediately beyond the rectory on the left. The signs for The Blackbird are visible just above the approaching car.

Looking west from NatWest Bank with the old West End smithy (now demolished) in use as a butchers on the left with Smith's Café (also demolished) at the entrance to the riverside park. On the opposite side, in the distance, is Ion's Café with Stobert's Supply Stores on the immediate right.

Main Street, seen from the rail bridge looking east, with West Farm on the right, in the 1950s. A number of the cottages on the left, before Neasham House, were demolished for the building of Merton Hall.

The demolition of Coates School in 1968 made way for the development of Coates Green in front of St Mary's. Note the entrance to Merton Way just before The Blackbird, which gave access to the new school, housing and shops in Thornhill Road.

The vicar's pele, c. 1900. This was the southern entrance wing to the old vicarage which was demolished in the 1860s when the new vicarage was built. The new vicarage (currently the divisional headquarters of Bellway Homes) was built under the guidance of the Alnwick architect F.R. Wilson.

The tower is believed to be thirteenth century in origin and this may account for the notes on the architect's survey drawing of 1864 which refer to the 'Ancient Turris de Ponteland'. The decision was taken to retain it as a harness room to the new development but it is evident that its usefulness declined and gradually the structure deteriorated to its present ruinous state.

Two

War and Peace

In common with most Northumbrian villages, Ponteland suffered centuries of border conflict between England and Scotland and the marauding activities of the Reivers. Perhaps the first notable military event took place on 14 August 1244 with the signing of a 'Peace Treaty' between the warring nations. This is said to have been agreed through the mediation of Walter de Gray, Archbishop of York, in St Mary's church (although some references claim it was signed in Ponteland Castle) as the armies of Alexander II of Scotland and Henry III converged upon Ponteland. The peace between the two kingdoms was however only temporary and there are several subsequent recorded instances of military incursions across the Border in both directions.

In 1388 the Scots, under the command of James Earl of Douglas, invaded England, raiding parts of Northumberland and Durham. On their return north they were encamped outside the city walls of Newcastle and combat took place between the Earl of Douglas and Sir Henry Percy (Hotspur) in which Hotspur was unhorsed. Hotspur's indignation was complete when, snatching the Percy pennant, James declared he would return to Scotland and fly the pennant from his castle at Dalkeith. Sir Henry vowed he would not reach Scotland with the booty. Douglas departed for Scotland early on Tuesday 17 August, and en route to his fatal encounter with Hotspur at the Battle of Otterburn on 18 August, passed through Ponteland, attacked the 'castle' (now the Blackbird Inn), captured Sir Aymer de Athol, Lord of the Manor, and razed the property to the ground.

The subsequent international military events of the nineteenth and twentieth centuries, though remote from Ponteland, have probably had more of an impact upon the lives and fortunes of the majority of local people and it is to these that this section is dedicated.

In Loving Memory of
WILLIAM JAMESON
of PENTELANDS,
Private in the Imperial Yeomanry,
Killed in Action at Doorn River, South Africa,
on November 5th, 1900,
AGED 28 YEARS.

William Jameson, son of James and Barbara Jameson who owned the shop next to the Methodist church, was a Private in The Imperial Yeomanry during the Boer War. He was killed in action at Doorn River, South Africa in 1900 aged twenty-eight.

Edward Jameson, cousin to William, also served in the Boer War but returned home safely in 1902 at the end of hostilities.

Young Norman Cowan (centre) enlisted as a trumpeter in the Northumberland Hussars in 1914 and after being trained for cavalry, the Hotchkiss gun and Mills bombs was sent to France in 1916. He was captured in 1918 and held as a prisoner of war until his repatriation in 1919.

Mr and Mrs Felix Morris, *c.* 1915. Mrs Morris (*née* Lyd Taylor) was a barmaid at The Seven Stars.

Corporal John Rea Jackson, blacksmith of Milbourne, served in the Territorial Army during the First World War. His active campaign for council housing in Ponteland was in due course recognised and Jackson Avenue was named after him. In 1926 he emigrated to Alberta in Canada, with his wife Annie and nine children, and settled in the small town of Sundre near Calgary. The Jackson Boy Scout Troop was subsequently established in honour of his service to his adopted community.

2nd Lieutenant Charles Frederick Jameson (13th Battalion Yorkshire Regiment) was one of two Ponteland men to be awarded the Military Cross for gallant conduct. His courage during an enemy attack on 17 March 1919 on Sred Mekrenga in Northern Russia was also recognised by the Russian Government with the award of the Royal Order of St Ann. The other MC was awarded independently to William March.

Augustine Hogg, a Dominican and son of R.P. Hogg, licensee of The Seven Stars, was a forces chaplain during the First World War

Lance Corporal Henry Bewick Stobert, grandson of James Stobert the 'Grand Old Man' of Ponteland Methodism.

PONTELAND

On Wednesday, June 19th, 1918,
a

SALE OF WORK

will be held at

THE CANTEEN.

The Sale will be opened by

Mrs. H. MIDDLETON,

BELSAY CASTLE,

at 2-30 p.m.

Proceeds will be divided between a War Memorial Fund, and a Fund to provide Materials for Soldier's Comforts.

TEA AT MODERATE PRICES.

ADMISSION FREE.

T. PEARSON, PRINTER & STATIONER, WEST ROAD, PONTELAND.

The Sale of Work was one of many fund raising events held in the village either to support the Armed Forces during hostilities or to commemorate their sacrifice afterwards. The articles sold were produced by the sewing parties organised by Mrs Tryphena Langton (the vicar's wife) and raised the sum of £63 towards the provision of a permanent war memorial and soldiers comforts. The canteen was in the cyclists' meeting house (see p. 4).

The Welcome Home Committee under the chairmanship of Revd F.W. Langton prepared a commemorative booklet, which together with a leather wallet, was presented in grateful recognition of Gallant Services rendered in the First World War. The Roll of Honour included 37 men who had died; of the 120 who returned 102 attended the reception. They also paid tribute to Thomas Weightman and James Stobert who had subsequently died of their wounds, and to those comrades who were buried abroad.

1914 - 1918

Ponteland and District Welcome Home

The Committee desire the pleasure of

Mr C. J. Jameson's

Company to Supper in Coates' Endowed School, and afterwards to Social (Dancing, etc.) in the Council School, on Friday, October 17th, 1919.

Supper at 6.30 p.m.

Social and Presentations at 8 p.m.

GAVIN WADE, HON. SECRETARY, PONTELAND.

R.S.V.P. NOT LATER THAN OCTOBER 13TH.

In 1919 a Peace Sports Event was organised by a Ladies Committee and the procession assembled outside the rectory.

The procession proceeded through the village past The Seven Stars.

The procession returns and we have a glimpse of the rail bridge in the background and the oriel window of the vicar's pele through the trees.

The celebrations culminated with a grand bonfire on Mr Stephenson's field at Eland Green Farm.

The memorial was built by public subscription and unveiled by Colonel Riddell in 1920, two years before the Memorial Hall opened. The railway signal and embankment can be seen in the background.

Prestwick Colliery Home Guard in 1941. From left to right, back row: -?-, Gordon Taylor (aged 16), -?-, Buck Graham, Tommy Strangeways, George Barras, Reggie Graham, Billy Weatman. Centre: Cyril Graham, -?-, Jackie Coulsen, Wilson Scott, Robbie Graham, Jack Lynch (aged 17). Front: John Guy, Mick Lynch (aged 16), Stan Taylor, Ronnie Lynch, Tommy Winthrop, Tucker Robson, Stan Simpson.

Ponteland Platoon of The Home Guard.

Revd Jackie Charlton Blackburn, Methodist minister, in unfamiliar attire, *c.* 1941.

Observer Corps on station at Berwick Hill under the command of J. Jameson who is seated second from the right.

Corporal Jack Thompson RAF (standing left), in 1940, with Tommie, Big Bill, Jimmie, Harry and Alex, some of the many Forces personnel entertained by Ponteland families during the Second World War. Jack married Doreen Stobert in 1941.

The demolition, in 1961, of Prisoner of War Camp No. 69, which was built in the early 1940s on Lot Nos. 152-155 (covering approximately twenty acres) between The Rise and Western Way, Darras Hall. Houses on Middle Drive and Western Way can be seen in the background. (Photo Ref. NRO444/17/2 courtesy of Northumberland County Record Office.)

POW No. B33675, Frank O. Brinkmann, was the German interpreter at the camp.

At the end of the war POWs were employed on local farms to make up for the labour shortage. This scene, at Harry Alder's Woodhill Farm in 1946, shows Hazel Earl and her mother Lizzie at harvest time with POWs Peter Peterson (left) and Franz ?

In 1952 Hazel Earl married Jackie Whitehead. Otto Schlien (left), who had been a POW at Camp 69 from 1943 to 1946, was best man and was granted British citizenship in 1953/54. He lived in Walridge until his death in 1987. Hazel was appointed Inaugural President of Thornhill Womens Institute in 1982, but now lives in Alnwick.

Veterans from the Second World War assemble at the Leisure Centre for the VE Day Parade in 1995. From left to right: Squadron Leader Fred Sealey (RAF), Flight Lieutenant Tom Hughes (RAF), Leading Aircraftswoman Dulcie Dytham (WAAF), Captain Harry Earp (Green Howards) and For'ard Gunner Stuart Oliver (RNVR).

After celebrating his 100th birthday, in October 1998, First World War veteran Norman Cowan was awarded France's highest honour at a special ceremony in the leisure centre in December 1998. Norman, seen here with his friend and companion Lilian Smith, was presented with the Légion d'Honneur by Dr Andrew Robinson, Honorary French Consul to the North of England.

Three

The Railway

Unlike some of the more remote areas of the North of England, which had experienced the full impact of the Industrial Revolution, travel and transportation of goods to and from Ponteland in the early 1800s was limited to horse-drawn vehicles. This was not unusual for a rural area though it was out of phase with some of the more remote communities, for example Alston in Cumbria which was already benefiting from direct railway links in 1852. The motivation for such development was of course the insatiable demand for resources to support the Industrial Revolution.

Pressure, however, began to build up from less obvious quarters and in 1896, in response to the proposed Light Railways Act, the County Surveyor to Northumberland County Council submitted a report to the Council Parliamentary Committee, stressing the urgent need for the provision of light railways. 'The increased use of heavy traffic on County Roads by farmers and others was placing a serious financial burden, on the ratepayers at large, for their repair and maintenance. Such traffic could be dealt with more economically by being diverted onto light railways'. Plans for such a light railway from South Gosforth to Scots Gap, via Woolsington, Ponteland, Saugh House, Old Deanham and Wallington had been prepared by the county in 1885 and it was resolved that the North-Eastern and North British Railways Companies be approached to ascertain their interest.

The Light Railways Act, finally introduced by the Government in 1896, made provision for expediting the administrative procedures for such large construction projects and for avoiding the costly Parliamentary applications. This was designed to encourage the construction of economical light railways in sparsely populated areas thereby drawing population from the overcrowded towns and cities. Applications were to be considered by a committee of three commissioners who had authority to make draft Orders for confirmation by the Board of Trade on behalf of Parliament.

In 1897 at the nineteenth half-yearly meeting of shareholders of the North-Eastern Railway Company the Chairman Sir Joseph W. Pease proposed two experimental light railway schemes 'to be solved by practice'. The first was the '12.5 mile North Holderness Light Railway through a purely excellent agricultural area' and the second was the '7 mile Gosforth to Ponteland Light Railway to be constructed through charming residential country'.

The Public Enquiry into the proposal was held in the boardroom at Central Station, Newcastle, on 19 May 1899. Lord Jersey (chairman to the commissioners) recommended that the Order be granted to construct a low cost rail link from the existing electrified loop at South Gosforth to Ponteland, via Kenton Bank Foot and Woolsington at an estimated cost of £33,398.

Looking north, *c.* 1900, behind the Main Street from a position which would now be on Darras Road. The cottage in the left foreground is that seen earlier, on page 22. Stobert's Supply Stores can be seen on the extreme left. The river Pont makes its way through the low ground beyond the greenhouse.

Preparatory work is in progress in 1904 behind West Farm (now Safeway) for construction of the railway over the Pont.

Construction of the twin arch bridge over the river.

Construction of the abutments to carry the railway over Main Street.

Looking east along Main Street with construction of the bridge abutments almost complete. The entrance to the tea rooms next to The Seven Stars can be seen in the right background and Neasham House is to the left.

Testing the temporary supports. Jimmy Hardman ('Coffee Tommy') stands just to the left of the horse. J. Lant (builder) walks from right to left and is dressed in a light suit.

Construction is complete on the new bridge carrying the rail track over Main Street.

The railway has arrived at Ponteland. A view to the east shows the embankment and the bridge over the river, with the old footbridge to the greenhouses (seen in the above photograph) shown in the foreground. This is the line of the present Darras Road bridge.

Ponteland station in 1905. This occupied the area that was subsequently used for part of the Merton Way shops and rear car park. The Meadowfield Industrial Estate was built on the adjoining rail marshalling area, which was described at the time as 'being constructed in expectation of considerable traffic'.

The first passenger train No. 1019 arrives at Ponteland station on 1 June 1905. The extension to Darras Hall was not built until 1913 and this was further extended in 1927 out to Mount Huly.

44

Stationmaster Collins and staff, *c.* 1930. Although the line closed to regular passenger traffic in 1929 it continued in casual use until it was finally closed in the late 1960s. The clock now hangs in The Diamond.

The line was used on several occasions as an overnight halt for members of the royal family visiting the North East. On this occasion, in 1939, King George VI and Queen Mary were touring in the area.

The level crossing at Callerton Lane in 1955.

The bridge over Main Street, seen here in 1960 from West Road, was subsequently demolished. The only remaining evidence of the railway is the route of the track and the remnants of the embankments.

Four
The Cottage Homes

Towards the latter part of the nineteenth century there was a general realisation of the growing need to provide orphans and other 'institutional children' with home life training. In 1895, at a meeting of The Guardians of the Poor of Newcastle Poor Law Union, it was resolved that arrangements should be made to remove children from the influences of life in the workhouse and to protect them from exploitation. Consequently in October 1897 a deputation of six Board members of The Guardians was delegated to visit Cottage Homes for children which had already been established throughout the country and report their findings and recommendations.

They visited Cottage Homes in the Kent, Worcestershire, Wolverhampton, Kings Norton, Leicester and Hunslet Unions and in December of that year the Board agreed to accept their recommendation to proceed with Cottage Homes for The Newcastle Union based upon the Hunslet model. A subcommittee was subsequently appointed and charged with the task of preparing the necessary details and the selection of an appropriate site for the approval of the Board.

John Leeson of Oliver, Leeson and Wood, Pilgrim Street, Newcastle upon Tyne, was subsequently appointed architect for the preparation of the necessary plans and contract documents for the construction of the complex, and in May 1899 it was resolved to purchase seventy acres of land at Smallburn Farm, Ponteland from Mr Alder.

The proposed development, in accordance with the Hunslet model, made no provision for the education of the children, other than infants; the burden of this was to fall on schools in the village. This was not well received by the vicar, the Parish Council, the Trustees of Higham Dykes School or Newton Ogle of Kirkley who were all concerned about the effect on the limited local school facilities.

The initial estimate of cost of the building work was £27,100 but following subsequent paring of the proposals this was reduced to £19,623 and in November 1899 the decision was finally taken to proceed. Tenders were invited for the work which was awarded, in March 1901, to E. Henderson and Son of Ponteland for the sum of £20,050 with a completion period of twenty-one months. In January 1903 early occupation was granted for some staff while work continued to final completion later that year at a final cost of £29,477.

Entrance to the Cottage Homes from the Kirkley Road, with the schoolhouse to the left and the Lodge on the right.

The Lodge, seen from the grounds of the Homes.

The schoolhouse.

In 1903 the Board of Guardians appointed Mr F.R.J. Harris, from Hounslow in Essex, to the position of First Superintendent to the Cottage Homes.

The Masters House, Lodge and schoolhouse.

F.R.J. Harris was accompanied by his wife Julia.

The children were accommodated in family groups in separate semi-detached homes under the supervision of housemothers.

The superintendent's house, with a water tower under construction in the background. Borehole drilling on site had secured a plentiful artesian supply of water.

F.R.J. Harris (seated in the centre) and staff are pictured, *c.* 1905.

Francis Harris died in September 1919 and a sundial was erected in the grounds in his memory. He was succeeded by his wife, Julia, who was matron.

Miss Margaret Helen Hindmarsh was a housemother in the 1920s.

Julia, as matron, was assisted by her son Frank. He is seen here standing to her right in the centre of the back row of this late 1920s staff photograph. On the back row, Mr Spinks is on the extreme left, Mr Bell is to the left of Frank Harris and Mr Frazer is next but one on the right. Miss Heron is seated third the from right in the centre row.

The 'Old Codgers' from the CTC assemble outside the smithy in the 1940s, in readiness for their annual visit to entertain the children at the Cottage Homes.

Staff in the 1940s, with Frank Harris on the extreme right and Mr Bell seated in the centre.

Housemother, Mary Brady, now Mrs Mary Craven, is pictured with her children in the early 1950s.

Mary Brady with her older children, outside No. 7.

On his retirement in 1952 Frank Harris was presented with a clock and a print of the famous Sir Peter Scott painting 'Geese in Flight'. Margaret Dodd, now Mrs Margaret Robinson, left the Homes in 1947 but returned for the retirement presentation. She is standing third from the right with her arm resting on the painting. (Photograph by kind permission of *Newcastle Evening Chronicle*.)

The former housemother, Margaret Ellen Hindmarsh, in 1955. She died in 1971 aged eighty-seven.

Five

The Churches

The oldest church in the village is St Mary's, dedicated to the Blessed Virgin and originally built in the late twelfth century. Substantial parts of the Norman structure still exist today – the most notable being the zigzag-arched west door.

Close links with Merton College, Oxford may be traced back to the 'Peace Treaty' of 1244 and one of Henry III's secretaries, Walter de Merton, who was responsible in 1274 for the foundation of Merton's House of Scholars at Oxford. In 1262 the then Lord of Ponteland (Baron Mitford) Roger Bertram III, exchanged some areas of land with Peter de Montford and disposed of others to raise money. In 1264 he was associated with Peter de Montford and other rebel barons in the rebellion against Henry III, which was crushed in 1265. To secure his pardon Roger forfeited his holdings to Henry's half brother, William de Valence, from whom the baronetcy ultimately passed by marriage in 1325 to the Earl of Athol who assumed the title Lord of Ponteland. Meanwhile in 1258 William de Merton, highly regarded by Henry, had been appointed Chancellor and to regain the King's favour Peter de Montford granted his land in Punt Eylaund to Merton's House of Scholars.

Early accounts of the beginnings of Methodism in Ponteland have their roots in an article which was first published in the 1898 winter edition of The Methodist Recorder. The reported interview with James Stobert, miller and farmer, attributed the birth of Methodism in the village to the arrival of his father and uncle in 1801. This anecdotal evidence has not been corroborated by recent research which indicates that the first dissenting certificate, to licence a gathering for worship outside the Established Church was issued to Thomas Lumsden in 1814. With this authority, Thomas was permitted to hold religious meetings in his West Road smithy. Furthermore available evidence suggests that the Stobert brothers were not resident in the village until around 1817.

James, born in 1825 and one of twin sons to Henry and Eleanor Stobert, did apparently attend his first Sunday school in 1828 and this would mark the beginning of a personal committment which was to link the Stobert family with Ponteland Methodism for the next 140 years or so. In 1839, on his first visit to Ponteland, Revd Joseph Fowler suggested the construction of a new chapel and this prompted Mr Reay of Kenton, who had just bought a farm near the village, to offer a site. This was accepted and the opening services were held in the new chapel on Good Friday, 1841.

Following the Reformation, followers of the Catholic faith were severely persecuted and there are many recorded instances of the brutal execution of priests and their protectors. The faith was kept alive in the parish by the Riddells of Cheeseburn Grange, their forbears and the Swinburne family of Capheaton. There were chapels and priests at both places but only the chapel at Cheeseburn, designed by John Dobson and built in 1820, survives. It was from this chapel that Ponteland was served with Mass being said in rented cottage accommodation in the West End and in Annie Fell's cottage next to Neasham House.

The 1662 Act of Uniformity separated Presbyterianism from the Established Church and, like the Catholics, many Presbyterians continued to worship in secrecy. This was so widespread that all assemblies of more than five persons for religious purposes, other than in accordance with the Church of England, were declared illegal. Following the 1688/89 Revolution, when James II was replaced by his sister Mary and William of Orange, an era of tolerance began and Meeting Houses were licensed for worship. It was not however until 1828 that all the Acts against Nonconformity were repealed. There are early references to Presbyterian meetings taking place at Kirkley and in the home of Mr A. Badenoch in the late 1880s. In 1929 the Newcastle Presbytery arranged for Sunday afternoon worship in the Memorial Hall but this was subsequently abandoned in 1935 through lack of support. The establishment of a Presbyterian church in Ponteland was again considered in 1962 and following a series of successful meetings of local interested people and the availability of the disused railway station building at Darras Hall the decision was taken to lease it for a regular meeting place. The first service was held on 15 December 1963.

An early photograph of St Mary's before the tower was buttressed on the south-west corner, the roof raised and the clock lowered to its present position. The church was closed during 1881 for these major works.

An early twentieth-century view with the buttress in place and showing the repositioned clock and new roof.

Revd Langton with Mrs Langton and daughters outside the new vicarage, built in 1864. He served the parish for thirty-nine years, from 1895 until his retirement in 1934.

The church of the Holy Saviour at Milbourne was built in 1868, by Miss Jane Ann Bates of Milbourne Hall, as a chapel-of-ease to St Mary's.

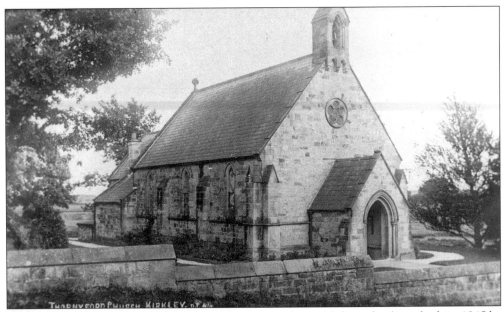

The chapel of St Barnabas at Thorneyford (just across the parish boundary) was built in 1845 by Revd J.S. Ogle.

On Christmas morning in 1929 a special service was held in the chapel to unveil the new window commissioned by Sir William Noble depicting the inter-denominational character of the Sunday night services. The artists were Mr J. Wilson Jowsey and Miss Jean Beckett, and the window was crafted by Messrs Reed Millican & Co.

The first Methodist church, built in 1841, is under threat from the river in flood in 1903. Robert Charlton rests at the end of the bridge.

In 1898 James Stobert, miller and farmer, was presented with a portrait photograph by the Methodist Circuit Local Preachers, in recognition of the work he had done for the church.

In 1904 the decision was taken to build a new Methodist chapel and finally, in 1907, building began on the site of the existing church. During construction services were held in the warehouse belonging to Henry Stobert (James' son) which adjoined the west-end shop. James died in 1905 and did not witness this great achievement. The later extension to the rear, built in 1927, can be clearly seen.

One of the foundation stones to the Methodist Church Hall extension in 1956 was laid, on behalf of the trustees, by Mr H.B. Stobert – grandson to James. His daughter Doreen, grand-daughter Liz and Revd Albert Gibbins witnessed the proud event. Bill Tait, headmaster at the 'top' school, looks on in the background.

The second foundation stone was laid by Mr Tom Straughan, on behalf of S. Harrison Smith, with Sid Courtney recording the commentary.

Prestwick Methodist church was built in 1882 and demolished in the 1960s, to make way for the construction of Woodlands, the home of Mr and Mrs Michael Taylor. The original foundation stones can be seen in the boundary wall to the new house and the old boiler house basement forms a very unusual water feature in the front garden.

Milbourne Methodist church was built in 1903 and is still in use today.

Revd W.E. Baron, the Catholic chaplain at Cheeseburn Grange between 1883 and 1892 is seen here accompanied by his housekeeper Grace Learny travelling out to Ponteland to celebrate Mass in a cottage in the village. The cottage is believed to have been occupied by the Smiths, who subsequently owned the café on the opposite side of West Road, at the entrance to the riverside park.

In 1901, shortly after he came to Cheeseburn, Father Henry Walmsley began to look for a more permanent site for a church in Ponteland and in 1903 the first church dedicated to St Matthew was opened in a wooden shed on the present site. This was in continuous use until 1947 when the congregation became too large for the accommodation.

In 1947 Father Leo Doyle became the last resident chaplain at Cheesburn and moved to Ponteland to plan for a new church. From 1947 until 1950, when the present church and presbytery were built, all services were held in Smith's Café which had been upgraded accordingly.

The opening of the new St Matthews was celebrated with Mass on Whit Monday in 1950. The old wooden shed was used by Father Doyle's housekeeper, Lucy McEvoy, as a hen house.

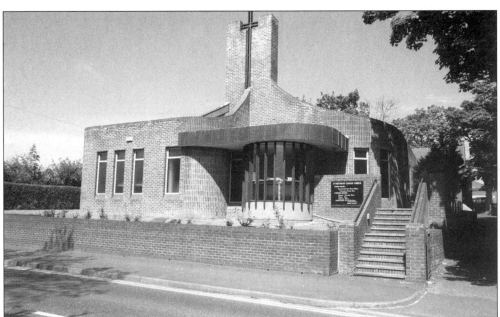

The church was further extended in 1978 to accommodate a growing Catholic population and in 1992 a new parish hall was built behind the church on the site of the original 1903 wooden hut.

The old Darras Hall railway station was leased from the Estate Committee in 1963 and after extensive repairs became the first established Presbyterian church in Ponteland.

Revd David Hannan was the first Presbyterian minister inducted in 1967 and he served the church through its formative years up to his retirement in December 1998.

The new United Reformed church, illustrated in this watercolour painting by the Revd Hannan, was dedicated in 1973. Additional accommodation was added in 1975 and 1983.

The old station building was demolished to make way for the Old Station Court housing development.

Six
The People

During any period of the history of a community it is interesting to examine the often significant and lasting contributions made by local families or individuals, to the general well-being and evolution of that community. These can so easily be forgotten, however, in Ponteland we are reminded frequently of our association with such people as Bell, Coates, Collingwood, Darras, Errington, Merton and others as these names have become part of our daily vocabulary. While most organizations, clubs or societies recognise unselfish contributions by giving special trophies or awards these people only receive recognition from a very limited cross section of the community.

In this section I have not set out to include every family or individual who has played a role in the development of the community. I have simply assembled a selection of people or families that I believe will compliment the rest of the publication. Some have very strong family links over very many years whereas others are relative newcomers.

Ponteland has an excellent reputation for the support of charitable fund-raising efforts held by numerous local organisations but it has not been physically possible to include them all. I hope those omitted will regard those included as adequate representation of their work.

No individual family has been particularly singled out; however it seems appropriate to highlight the failure to publicly recognise the vision and foresight of Joseph Whiteside Wakinshaw – the 'Father of Darras Hall', whose initial memorial was short-lived with the renaming of Old Station Court. Perhaps there is some consolation in believing that Runnymede Road was named after his home in Westerhope.

The Straughan family, c. 1890. From left to right, standing: Thomas (born 1874), John, Robert (born 1866), William (born 1876). Seated: James (born 1860), Isabella Davidson (born 1836), Adam (born 1863).

John and Annie Jameson, *c.* 1890.

Wedding of Joseph Henderson (builder) and Charlotte Alice on 8 April 1901.

From left to right: W. Barrons, R. Reay and Edward Henderson, *c.* 1901.

Margaret Berkley with her children at Bridge End, *c.* 1902. Her husband, Matthew Charlton Berkley, was a butcher.

The Berkley family group is pictured in the garden at the end of the shop.

The wedding of Joseph Henderson Jameson and Annie, in the early 1900s. James Jameson is to Annie's left.

The wedding of Edward Jameson and Hannah Caughey on 25 September 1906. Joe Henderson is third from right, James Jameson is in the centre and Edward Henderson is on the extreme left of the back row.

Edward Jameson talks to a delivery man (who may have been delivering coal), *c*. 1910. His mother, Annie, and wife, Hannah, stand at the front door to Annie's shop.

Miss Wilkinson prepares for a delivery of groceries for her father John Wilkinson, *c*. 1910.

The Hope twins, daughters of David Hope, are pictured outside their home in Bell Villas, *c.* 1910.

Joseph Henderson, *c.* 1910.

The O'Neal children in front of the west end cottages, *c.* 1905. These were subsequently demolished to provide access to the Meadowfield Industrial Estate. One of the cottages was The Windmill Inn.

Pictured from left to right are: Sarah, Ann and Robert Reay in front of College Row, *c.* 1905.

The Harrison girls entertain at Streethouses (now The Badger), *c.* 1908. George Harrison was a cattle dealer.

A group of miners at the shaft to the old Prestwick Land Sale Pit, *c.* 1900. James Taylor, seated on the extreme left, was a 'Master Sinker'.

Bill Taylor outside No. 1 Prestwick Square, c. 1913, which has survived the airport development. The tower for the aerial ropeway, which carried coal from the Dinnington and old Prestwick Pits to the Coal Preparation Plant at the new pit adjoining the railway at Prestwick Road end, is just in view to the extreme right.

Man of the road, Jimmy Hardman, c. 1910. He was affectionately known to children and many other locals as 'Coffee Tommy'. Jimmy slept at Kenton Millstone quarry but his 'beat' extended to Fawdon, Dinnington and Ponteland. It was believed that he was struck by a vehicle in a 'hit and run' incident, and he died in hospital in 1925.

The wedding of Henry (Harry) Bewick Stobert, grandson of James, and Lily Harris, daughter of Francis and Julia Harris in 1916.

From left to right: Billy Straughan, -?-, John Straughan and Kinston Straughan parade their horses behind West Farm, c. 1920.

In 1924 after the closure of the Spencer Steelworks at Newburn, the Harrisons moved from Walbottle and bought five acres of land at the north end of Western Way, Darras Hall to set up a nursery. Gordon, one of the two sons, is pictured making the concrete blocks for their bungalow adjoining the nursery.

Percy Rowell, choirmaster at Ponteland Methodist church in the 1930s.

Thomas Scott, stationmaster, *c*. 1933.

The Straughan family and friends in the 1930s. From left to right, back row: Jack, -?-, Flo, Billy, Thomas, Kingston, Peggy, Edna Marshall, Stewart Marshall (from Blyth) and Willie Short (from Powburn). Front: Mary, Bella.

Mrs Wadsworth (left) with Jessie Robinson (née Gilhespie) outside her shop in Main Street, mid-1930s.

An outing to Druridge Bay in the 1930s. Pictured are: Rowley Yates and daughter, Peggy Vincent, Mary Carss, Freda Gordon, Bessie Carss, Doreen Stobert.

Henry Stobert, Tom Straughan, James Jameson and other dignitaries lead the parade in celebration of the Coronation of King George VI.

James and Annie Taylor in their front garden at Prestwick Cottages, c. 1939. These were demolished in the 1960s to make way for The Airport Hotel.

James Jameson, who died in 1946. He had been president of Ponteland AFC, a founder member of Ponteland Golf and Bowling Clubs, and assistant secretary to Ponteland Floral & Horticultural Society (for forty-five years). He trained Volunteers in the First World War, led the Observer Corps during the Second War, and held the post of surveyor to Castle Ward Union from 1904 to1939. He died at the age of seventy-eight.

Postman Lewis Pearson and Nancy Blaylock (*née* Harrison) supervise Jack Harrison and Eric Charlton snow clearing in February 1947, outside the Harrison's nursery on Western Way.

Harry and Lily Stobert with the staff inside the West End Supply Stores, c. 1950. Jack Thompson is in the background with, from left to right: Dulcie Bright, Lily Armstrong, Harry, Joan Sloan, Lily, Rose Eaton, Evelyn Hogarth, Elsie Foster.

Wedding of Tom Harrison and Joan Hallett at The Wagon in 1953. Imagine strolling across the A696 today!

Two generations of Moorheads: Jack and his father outside the smithy, c. 1950.

The late Bobby Cowell came to Ponteland following his enforced retirement, in 1956, from a magnificent football career with Newcastle United. Legendary figures such as Scoular, Milburn, Mitchell, Shackleton, Lawton, Carter, Matthews, Shankley and Doherty played in his testimonial in 1956.

Founder officers of Rotary Club of Ponteland, which held its Charter Meeting in the Memorial Hall in December 1964. From left to right: John Hetherington (junior vice-president), Colin Watkins (treasurer), Kingsley Longstaff (president), John Waggott (senior vice-president), Bernard Long (secretary).

Geoff Warner outside his shop in Main Street, 1968 or '69. Note the demolition of the adjoining property to make way for the construction of Midland Bank.

Gordon Harrison admires 'Walbottle' – one the many daffodil varieties he bred and named after local towns and villages. Gordon, who died shortly after this photograph was taken in 1971, was also a member of the Alpine Society. His garden at 41 Western Way was listed with the Northumberland County Gardens Scheme. (Photograph by kind permission of *Garden News*.)

Bernard Long, Jack Heron and Mrs Ann Bowman (of the NSPCC) examine the Rotary toy collection. Started by Jack and his late wife Masie in 1977 it is now an established part of the annual Rotary fund-raising programme. This culminates in the very popular Christmas carol service in the Memorial Hall with The Bedlington Salvation Army Band.

Parish Council chairman Lindley Dewhirst presents Dick Dodsworth with the Parish Council Challenge Rose Bowl at the second Annual Parish Flower and Vegetable Show in 1979. The show was revived in 1978, after a break of over twenty years, by Dr Jack White and a committee of local people. Bob Woolley (chairman of the committee) and his wife, May, watch the proceedings.

Stan Dytham, the late Bobby Thompson and Bill Crowe examine the winning blooms at the Northumbria Police Annual Flower Show in 1981 or '82. All three were very popular local judges, although on this occasion it is likely that the judging was by Stan. Bobby (a national rose breeder) was head gardener at police headquarters and Bill was a police inspector at Morpeth before he retired to his nursery at Scots Gap.

Hew Wright, from Care Village, prepares a delivery from Jack Thompson's bakery, *c.* 1985.

The late Bob Woolley, -?-, and May Woolley. Bob initiated the Northumbria in Bloom competition in 1965 and was chairman until his death in 1992. He was a founder member and chairman of the Annual Parish Flower Show and a member of the North of England 'Rosecarpe' Society. May succeeded Bob as chair to Northumbria in Bloom and holds that position today.

Dr Jack White, Mrs Ann Harrison (British Red Cross), and the late Barbara White relax in their garden at Bridge House which is open to visitors in aid of the British Red Cross Society. Jack is a former parish councillor, and founder, past chairman and current president of the Ponteland Parish Flower and Vegetable Show. Barbara was an active member of the show committee.

Mrs Kitty Slessor, wife of the late PC Slessor.

Ronnie Blench, the familiar figure responsible for maintaining Coates Green and other areas in Ponteland.

Ossie Robson on his daily visit to Ponteland from Medburn.

Seven

Sport and Leisure

While the churches and schools have always played an important role in village life it is interesting to observe the changes in sporting and leisure activities as society has become more affluent, has developed wider interests and has more time available to pursue them. The lack of suitable facilities has seldom been a deterrent – several activities have flourished and succeeded against all odds. This is certainly true in the later quarter of the 1800s when the football and cricket teams and the Ponteland Floral and Agricultural Society were formed. Despite having no fixed venues for many years they thrived and developed into major leisure activities in the village. Such success is clearly attributable to the commitment and dedication of the people involved and the encouragement and support from others.

The encouragement for founding the Ponteland Football and Cricket Clubs came from an unlikely source in Miss Holt, choirmistress of St Mary's church. In 1880 she encouraged an eleven-year-old James Jameson, friends and fellow choristers to take up these activities. From the tender age of fourteen he assumed the captaincy – a position he was to retain for fifty years. While the Jameson Cup is a lasting memento to James' indisputable loyalty and commitment to the club, Miss Holt's contribution remains unheralded.

The first annual show of Ponteland Floral and Agricultural Society was held in August 1882 on Mr John Temperley's land in the village. In March 1889 the committee met in The Seven Stars under the chairmanship of Alexander Badenoch to confirm the venue for the 1889 show as a field belonging to Mr J. Robson of Clickemin Farm. The programme, which included a concluding ball, held in a 'tent', reflected the substantial agricultural and horticultural influence in the area. The music on this occasion was provided by the Newcastle Artillery Volunteer Band. The running expenses for the annual event certainly exceeded the income on the day and its continuing success in the early years relied upon the generosity of the growing number of society members, who were invariably those same people committed to the organisation of other village activities.

The annual event started around 1882 and was held every year until 1939, when it was abandoned through lack of support and the outbreak of the Second World War. It is ironic that by 1939 the show had established a more permanent location on land adjoining the Auction Mart.

Ponteland Cricket Club team, c. 1904. From left to right, standing: James Jameson (captain), Joe Jameson, -?-, J. Bates, -?-, Joe Henderson. Seated: J. Caughey, E. Henderson, W.F. Fatkin, W. Barron, J. Brown, T. Atkinson.

Ponteland Football Club team, *c.* 1904. James Jameson is at the extreme left of the back row and Edward Jameson is on the right of the centre row.

Facilities for some activities, such as croquet, were provided at the vicarage.

Tennis courts were available at the vicarage and Revd Langton encouraged their use.

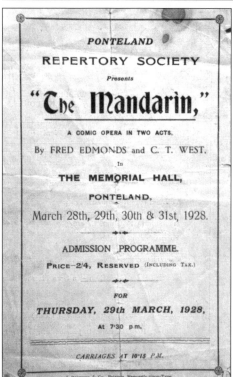

PONTELAND

REPERTORY SOCIETY

Presents

"The Mandarin,"

A COMIC OPERA IN TWO ACTS.

By FRED EDMONDS and C. T. WEST,

In

THE MEMORIAL HALL,

PONTELAND,

March 28th, 29th, 30th & 31st, 1928.

ADMISSION PROGRAMME.

PRICE—2/4, RESERVED (INCLUDING TAX.)

FOR

THURSDAY, 29th MARCH, 1928,

At 7·30 p.m.

CARRIAGES AT 10·15 P.M.

J. Bowman & Co., Printers, Newcastle-upon-Tyne.

The opening of the Memorial Hall on 20 December 1922, encouraged the formation of the Bowling Club in 1923 and the Repertory Society, which held its first performance in March 1928.

The Ponteland Golf Club, established on land leased from Mr Meek of Eland Hall Farm, was opened in 1928 by Lord Ridley, the taller of the men standing in the centre behind the trophies. Mr W. Nunn, the first chairman, stands to his immediate right and Revd Langton is third to his left. Mr James Jameson is seated on the second row, third from the right.

By 1931 the second nine holes were established and the extended course was opened by Lord Kirkley, seated centre, with his wife to his right and W. Nunn to his left.

The committee of the Agricultural & Horticultural Society (incorporating the Clydesdale Horse Society), *c.* 1930. From left to right, back row: -?-, Dr Holmes, T. Berkley, E. Jameson. Centre: W. Ridley, J. Moffat, J. Potts, -?-, W. Wilson, G. Clark, T. Field, -?-, R. Reay, R. Charlton. Front: R.L. Jobling, Revd Langton, Lord Ridley, J. Elliot, J. Jameson, J. Henderson and C.F. Jameson.

It wasn't until 1934 that the Bowling Club had the facility of a clubhouse, opened by Mr James Hilton. (Photograph by kind permission of *The Newcastle Journal*.)

In 1937 the new clubhouse for the golf course, built by Thomas Hutchinson & Co. at a cost of £4,000, was opened by club president Mr C.D. Beane. The club finally purchased the land for the course in 1947.

Competitors enter the arena for the riding events in the Annual Agriculture Show in 1938. (Photograph courtesy of *The Sunderland Echo*.)

Preparing for the 1938 production of *Rose of Persia*. From left to right: Frank McArdle, Doreen Stobert, Doris Chapman, Mary Carss, Kathleen Armstrong (*née* Carss), Tom Shield.

An impromptu rehearsal outside the Memorial Hall in 1938. Hassan (Jim Caddick), Sultan (Phil Waddle) and Abdallah (Brian Armstrong) are pictured.

Ponteland United Football Club, *c.* 1948. From left to right, standing: Billy Abbey, Billy Hepple, -?-, -?-, -?-, Jack Johnstone, Les Johnstone (goalkeeper), Leo Johnstone, -?-, Rod Lynch, Billy Wilkinson -?-, -?-. Kneeling: Frank Lynch, -?-, -?-, -?-, -?-.

In September 1947 the Bowling Club won the Edwardson Cup 92-53 in the final match against Brighton BC. From left to right, standing: R. Meek, J. Neal, J. Moorhead, W. Hepple, A. Walker, C.F. Jameson, R. Yates, J. Oliver, T. Fatkin, E. Morley and E. Forster. Seated: W. Reed, K. Straughan, R. Pascoe (treasurer), E. Stokoe (secretary), W. Barrons (chairman), J. Carr (assistant secretary), J.H. Hall, H.B. Stobert, J. Robson. Front: M. (Pat) Johnstone, W. Urwin.

Ponteland has always been a very popular venue for cyclists, seen here passing along the West Road, past Ion's Café on the left, in the late 1940s. The old railway bridge can be seen in the background.

Len Shackleton XI in a charity cricket match against a T.G. Hogarth XI at Kirkley in the early 1950s. Len Shackleton is standing fourth from the left and John Marshall is the umpire, on the right.

Thomas George Hogarth XI. From left to right, standing: T.G. Hogarth (with hat), Dalton Hutchinson, Jim Jameson, -?-, -?-, Joe MacDonald, George Walton, Ian Jordan, Isaac Batey (umpire). Kneeling: Benny Minto, -?-, John Parker, Jack Halliwell, Louis Robson.

Ponteland United pre-match against Gateshead Reserves at Redheugh Park in 1971. From left to right, back row: -?-, George Leadbetter, Bobby Frazer, Derek Brown, George Pilkington, Frank Leadbetter. Front: -?-, Andy Lockey, Brian Everett, Barry Cowell, John Cowan, Bobby Cowell.

Ponteland Bowling Club in 1976. From left to right: Tom Martin (club champion), Tom McPhee (Milne rose bowl winner) and John English (two bowl champion).

Twenty-fifth anniversary of The Blackbird Annual Leek Show, in 1981. From left to right: Charlie Ions, David Marshall, Stuart Ransome, Billy Abbey, Frank Smith, Billy Watson, Bill Dixon, John Marshall, Eric Royle, Peter Hyman, Gerald Ions.

Ponteland Cricket Club First Team 1991. From left to right: Jeff Oliver, Lindsey Bray, John Kirton, Jonathan Horrocks, Mike Lynch, Andrew Morgan, Bill Roddam, Brett Elliott, Richard Welbury, Bernie Jones, Ron Fairweather.

Annual Parish Flower Show class winners in 1991. From left to right: Tom Hughes, David Goodchild, Adam Wilkinson, Dorothy Warner, Pauline Lund, Dulcie Dytham, Jack White, Joan Harrison, Garry Blessed, Irene Cassidy. In front are Tanya and Crystal Courtney.

Competitors ready for off in the annual seven furlong wheelbarrow race (here in 1995) which is held each New Years Day. Its origins are uncertain though the old Annual Agricultural Show did include a similar event.

Preparing for the start of the Rotary Club duck race on the Pont in 1996. From left to right: Bill Boone, Bob Crosbie, Charlie Laidlaw, Ron Moore, Peter Burnett, Bill Hayhurst, Derek Boothby, Ian Cooper, Hugh McCambridge, Robbie Robson (president), Neil Mackley, Mark Havery, John Bromley, Alan Thompson, Crosbie Bryson, Dick Dodsworth, Trevor Bourn, Graham Shepley, Donald Elsmore.

Eight
The Younger Generation

Early schools were very dependent upon the public-spirited acts of reformers of the time or the generosity of local people who had a social conscience and the necessary resources for their continuing support and upkeep.

Richard Coates of Horton Grange died in 1719 in Newcastle and in his will made provision for the erection and endowment of a school in Ponteland to accommodate fifteen or more poor children of the parish. The school, built in 1727 on the site currently occupied by an estate agent, was financed in its entirety by the income from his estate, which also financed the grey school uniforms. The affairs of the school were administered by trustees appointed under the terms of the will who were also charged with the responsibility for the appointment of master. During the course of the next 150 years or so the school was rebuilt and altered several times to satisfy the growing demand for additional accommodation. By 1873 rebuilding of the school for 175 pupils was already in progress on a new site immediately in front of St Mary's church. The land was conveyed '…freely and voluntarily…' to the trustees by the Merton school of Scholars '…without valuable consideration…'. The new school was built in 1874 and Mr and Mrs Nield took up their appointments as master and teacher on 5 April 1875. The endowment provided free education for the poor children only and towards the latter part of the nineteenth century fees for others ranged from one shilling per quarter for the under fives to eight shillings for twelve year olds, the latter being the school leaving age.

In 1890 the old Coates School building was converted into an institute, library and reading room available to all men and boys above the age of fourteen years who paid the annual fee of one shilling.

Miss Mary Cook Bell of Higham Dykes erected and endowed a small day and Sunday school in 1852 on land to the west of The Wagon. This building is currently a private house with an adjoining cattery. A similar building, for thirty pupils, was erected in 1861 by Newton Charles Ogle of Kirkley Hall on the north side of the road to Whalton and this building also survives today as a private residence.

In 1960 a third Coates Endowed School was built on Thornhill Road adjacent to the Queen Elizabeth Playing Fields, which had been established earlier in 1953 to commemorate the Coronation. The 'old' Coates Endowed School was demolished in 1968. Further schools were built in Darras Hall and Callerton Lane in the 1960s and '70s to meet the needs of the ever increasing population and after the 1972 re-organisation of the education system in the county the roles of the older village schools were changed.

The 'new' school, *c.* 1875. The church clock is at the top of the tower which has no buttress, and the church roof has a low pitch.

Mr Nield with pupils, *c.* 1890. He was headmaster at Coates School from 1874 until he died in 1898.

Coates School, group II, c. 1898. George Edward Henderson, standing on the extreme left was a pupil teacher at the school from the day after he left at twelve years old until he was twenty-one. He left to join his brother Joseph who had secured the contract to build the Cottage Homes.

Coates group VII, c. 1907. At the front are Kingston Bowring Straughan (left) and John Straughan (next to him). Peggy Straughan is second on the right from the teacher. Henry William Tustin, who was also organist and choirmaster at St Mary's, was headmaster until he died in 1920.

A new council (top) infant's school was built on North Road, *c.* 1910. This was to ease the burden of the growing population of the village and the increasing numbers of children from the Cottage Homes. It also provided an alternative to the church school. In this photograph from around 1917, Mary Straughan, pictured third from the right, and classmates prepare for a dancing lesson.

Entertainment for the wounded at Gosforth Hospital in 1917. From left to right, standing: -?-, -?-, Eva Green, Mollie Laws. Seated: Carmen Green, -?-, Victoria Dora May Green, -?-.

In April and December of 1923 Miss Heron from the Cottage Homes produced a juvenile operetta *Snow-white and the Little Dwarfs* in the Memorial Hall. The nine dwarfs are, from left to right: R. Hornby, G. Ions, S. Hall, P. Atkinson, V. Carss, E. Smith, S. Smith, N. Hope, G. Smith.

By 1925 the council school was attracting more pupils from Coates Endowed. John Carr is the headmaster and Wilfred Stanley Taylor is seated on the extreme right next to the teacher. Note the Cottage Homes ('homers') children with their distinctive collars. In 1932 the Coates School was to take on the role of infant and junior school and the 'top' school was to become the senior school, teaching children from eleven years to fourteen or fifteen.

Girl Guides camping at Belsay, *c.* 1920s. Eva Green is seated in the centre of the front row.

Local lads enjoy the hospitality of Lord Kirkley, as recorded by his grandson Miles Williamson-Noble, at a sports day at Kirkley Hall in 1931. Major Briggs was Lord Kirkley's secretary.

Children assemble outside the Coates Endowed School for a procession through the village in celebration of the Coronation of King George VI in 1937. Brian Jameson is sitting on the hobby-horse and Peter Jameson is dressed as a golly.

Almost ready to go! The Blackbird and The Blackbird Gardens can be seen in the background.

Pupils at Higham Dykes School, c. 1940. From left to right, back row: Dorothy Simpson, Joan Hallett, Doreen Reid, Jill Parker (evacuee) and Stuart ? (evacuee). Front: Edward Smith, Robert Reid, Gladys ? (evacuee), Joan Bell, Pippa Brown, Austin Dodds, Boyd Taylor.

Mr Reid, who normally emptied the earth closets at Higham Dykes School, is pictured with an unusual cargo outside The Wagon in the 1940s. From left to right: Joan Hallet, Sheila and Doreen Reid, -?-, Madge ?

114

Ponteland County Top School, winners of the Schools Country Dance and Singing Competition at the Newcastle City Hall in 1954. From left to right, boys: Michael Taylor, Robert Dimmick, Leslie Bolam, Donald Charlton, Teddy Stevenson, Billy Gallon, Peter Cutts. Girls: Dorothy Honeyset, Barbara Miller, Yvonne Railton, Elaine Stokoe, Margaret Young, Leslie Crabb, Joyce Ions, Verne Stewart, Maureen Gowland, Eileen Armstrong, Sheila Urwin, Ann Grey, Ann Forster.

Jimmy Hall, Scoutmaster to the 1st Ponteland Troop and Wolf Cub Pack, and his Scouters sit proudly amid 'The Gang' who presented a revue, *Spring,* in the Memorial Hall from 1-6 May 1961.

All dressed up in Kirkley Drive to celebrate the Queen's Jubilee.

Group of High School students on the gold expedition for The Duke of Edinburgh Award Scheme at Lockau Fada in the Torridon area in 1992. From left to right: Zoe Robinson, Amanda Gould, Carolyn Knight, Helen Flynn, Catherine Hamilton, Sophie Betts, Kate Baylis.

Nine

Kirkley Hall

Early records identify Kirkley as 'Crikelaw', owned by the de Ure family in the Baronetcy of Mitford. The estate was eventually acquired by the Ogles in 1632 and Cuthbert Ogle built the first Manor House on a site just to the south of the present structure. This manor was replaced in 1764 by a Hall built on the present site by the Revd Newton Ogle who was also responsible for the erection, in 1788-89, of the Obelisk which dominates the high ground, known as 'Monument Hill', to the south-west of the Hall. This monument celebrated the centenary of the succession of Mary and William of Orange and the beginning of the era of religious tolerance. Kirkley Hall was granted a magistrates licence as a Non-conformist meeting place and a purpose built meeting house was established at Thorneyford as a single-storey building on the north bank of the river Blyth to the east of the Morpeth road.

Revd John Sackville Ogle succeeded his father Newton in 1804 and in 1834 he carried out extensive alterations to the Hall and built the Main Gate and South Lodge. In 1845 he built St Barnabas chapel at Thorneyford on the opposite side of the road to Morpeth to the eighteenth-century meeting house which was subsequently converted to two-storey farm cottages. The chapel was provided for the use of the Church of England and the benefit of the inhabitants of the estate. The chapel itself was sold in the 1970s and converted into a residential dwelling.

In 1922 the Ogles disposed of the outlying areas of the estate and Sir William J. Noble, a successful Tyneside industrialist purchased the Hall and adjoining land. He was born in Newcastle in 1863 and became one of the most respected members of the British and international shipping industries. He held numerous positions in Tyneside industry, including the chairmanship of the Cairn Line of Steamships Ltd.

In a disastrous fire on 17 May 1929 the Hall was virtually destroyed. It was rebuilt under the guidance of the architect Burns-Dick and re-occupied by Sir William as Lord Kirkley after his elevation to the baronetcy in 1930. On his death in 1935 the estate was inherited by his daughter Mrs H.B. Williamson Noble, but was tenanted by Lady Redhead. In 1948 it was sold, for a little over £26,000, to Northumberland County Council to set up a Farm Institute.

Kirkley Hall Farm Institute opened in 1950 with Mr D. Elsmore as the first principal. It was renamed Northumberland College of Agriculture in 1968 when Mr P.W. Blake was appointed.

The original Hall as built by Revd Newton Ogle.

Sir William J. Noble, who became Lord Kirkley in 1930.

The Hall after it was rebuilt following the fire in 1929.

During the reconstruction Sir William and family moved out of Kirkley to live in Jesmond. Upon his return in 1930 as Lord Kirkley his estate workers welcomed him and, in a demonstration of their respect for him, towed his Rolls Royce up the long drive.

Mr Donald Elsmore, appointed in 1950, was the first principal.

The entrance to Kirkley Hall Farm Institute in 1950.

Provision was made for the ladies in agriculture with the traditional domestic science courses and the very popular 'Country Woman' course. Some of the first students are pictured around 1952. From left to right: -?-, -?-, Susanne Robinson, Sheila Loughler, Patricia Dent, -?-.

Early students with the Friesians, c. 1955. From left to right: Norman Empey, Don Potts (stockman), John Banks, Peter Strutt.

Donald Empey demonstrates the versatility of the old Fordson, *c.* 1955. Note the starting handle at the base of the radiator!

Threshing in the 1950s – quite different from today's work carried out by combine harvester. From left to right: Oscar Pearson, Alan Reay, John Banks, David Potts, Norman Empey (just visible), Peter Strutt.

Riddling potatoes, c. 1950. Left to right: -?-, Oscar Pearson, -?-, John Banks, David Hughes, John Stott. The student examining the drive has not been identified.

Winners of the inter-college Ploughing Competition in 1966. From left to right: Charles Carson, -?-, -?-, David Anderson, Bob Cowen.

Frank Harrington, a lecturer in Applied Agriculture until his retirement in 1996, is pictured in very unfamiliar attire! Frank is now a parish councillor and deputy mayor to Castle Morpeth Borough Council.

Staff and students in 1964/65. From left to right, staff: Bob Cowen, Marion Holmes, Charles Carson, Peter King, Miss Constantine, Robin Gill, Mrs Smith, P. Blake (vice principal), J. Hetherington (principal), M. Boothroyd, Miss Reay (matron), R. Neal, -?-, A. Hetherington, -?-, P. Green. Centre row, students: R. Sutton, I. Clayton, D. Atkinson, -?-, D, Hubb, P. Springett, R. Adams, C. Longhurst, -?-, E. Sharrett, K. Robinson, J. Armstrong, J. Lawie, S. Maughan, M. Hall, -?-. Back row, students: -?-, Beattie, J. Wardle, D, Fairless, -?-, G. Foukes, W. Johnson, P. Morrison, H. Emmerson, G. Taylor, M. Chinnery, P. Scott, A. Strachan, E. Stafford, J. Aynsley, J. Henderson, J. Metcalf, D. Curry, -?-.

Ten
Dissington Hall

In 1794 when the local architect William Newton was commissioned to design the Hall, the North and South Dissington townships were in Newburn parish, however, subsequent boundary adjustments annexed both to the Ponteland parish.

From the time of the Norman conquest these manors were part of the baronetcy of Seaton Delaval and it was Ralph Delaval who sold North Dissington to Edward Collingwood of Byker in 1673. South Dissington was at this time owned by a separate descendant of the Delavals, Sir Jacob Astley, who also disposed of his estate to Edward Collingwood. Presumably Collingwood wished to establish a 'county seat' in response to his earlier appointment, in 1699, as High Sheriff of Northumberland. He died in 1701 and it was yet another Edward Collingwood, cousin to the famous Lord Collingwood, who at the age of sixty appointed William Newton. Although the building was probably completed in 1797, Edward preferred to live at the family home at Chirton and when he died in 1806, without issue, he bequeathed Dissington Hall to Walter Stanhope of Canon Hall in Yorkshire, whose third son Edward Spencer Stanhope succeeded to the estate, subject to the proviso that he changed his name to Edward Collingwood. He complied and changed his name by deed poll when he came of age in 1817, and in 1868 the property descended to his sister Arabella, whose husband Robert Gordon Calthorp, vicar of Irton in Cumbria, also assumed the name of Collingwood. The estate remained in the Collingwood family until 1957, although it is evident that throughout the 160 years of their ownership they spent very little time in occupation.

Emerson Muschamp Bainbridge (founder of the Newcastle department store which carries his name today) leased Dissington Hall for about fourteen years in the mid-1800s. The Deuchar family held a long lease before the Second World War and during the war years the Royal Air Force and Army occupied the Hall, which for a period was used for ammunition storage. For the internal fabric of the building to survive 'arms-length' ownership for such long periods of time is very surprising and it is perhaps a reflection of the caring stewardship of the present owners that some of the original qualities have been restored and preserved.

The Church Commissioners acquired the estate in 1957 and it was subsequently broken up with the exception of the farms and woodland which were retained by the Commissioners. The walled garden and original garden house, now a substantial building, were separated from the Hall and immediate grounds. The latter were acquired in 1968 by Mr and Mrs Eric Brown who, with their son Michael and his wife Jill, have developed Dissington Hall into a premier venue for business conferences and promotions, functions, weddings and receptions.

The Hall, seen from parkland to the south.

The east wing was not part of the original building, it was not built until the 1830s.

The 'Imperial'
staircase as
described by
Pevsner 'with Ionic
columns on the
ground floor…'

The original games room in the east wing has been converted into a marriage suite and function
room.

The Hall was one of the venues used for the ITV adaptation of Catherine Cookson's *Black Velvet Gown*. Janet McTeer (Riah) and Bob Peck (Miller) make final preparations before the cameras roll.

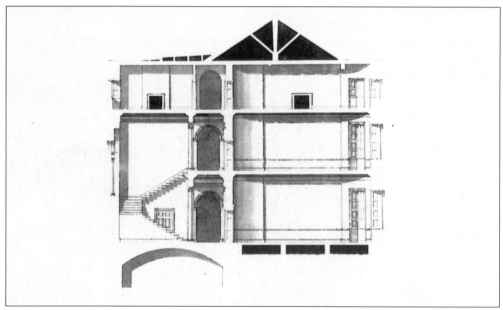

For many years the identity of the architect responsible for the design of the Hall was uncertain. In the 1970s a book of original plans annotated 'The Hall which was never built' were found in London and subsequent research established that these were the original architect's plans for Dissington Hall. This drawing signed by William Newton is one of that collection, it is a section through the main building, looking east.